Late for school

Story by Jenny Giles

Illustrations by Genevieve Rees

"Wake up, Nick!" said Mom.
"We are all very late."

"But I can't be late
for school today," said Nick.
"I have to play soccer.
Where are my shorts?"

3

"Help!" said Sarah.
"I can't find my socks."

"I have to go to work now,"
said Mom.
"Dad is making your breakfast."

"But we can't have breakfast,"
said Nick. "We are too late."

"Come on," said Dad.

"Have your breakfast.

Then I will take you to school

in the car."

"Oh, thanks, Dad,"

said Sarah and Nick.

"Thanks!"

Sarah and Nick had breakfast.

Then they ran out
to the garage with Dad.
They all got into the car.

"Let's go, Dad!" said Nick.

Rrrr ... rrrr ... rrrr
went the car.

"The engine is cold," said Dad.

"Oh, no!" cried Sarah.
"We are going to be so late!"

"Come on, car!" said Nick.
"Go! Go! GO!"

Brmmm! went the engine.
Brmmm! Brmmm!

"**Yes!**" shouted Nick.
"Now we can go!"

"But we are late for school,"
said Sarah.

They went down the street
in the car.

"Look!" said Nick.
"I can see some children
playing soccer.
The bell has not rung!"

"Oh, **good**!" said Sarah.
"We are not late for school
after all."